# TRAIL NOTES

BELONGS TO:

_____

IF FOUND, I MIGHT BE LOST, BUT TRY ME:

_____

_____

**TRAIL NAME**

**DATE**

**AREA**

**HIKING PARTNER(S)**

**MILEAGE**

**ELEVATION CHANGE**

**HIGH POINT**

**TRAILHEAD GPS COORDINATES**

**TRAIL AND WEATHER CONDITIONS**

**SPOTTED ALONG THE WAY**

**GENERAL NOTES**

**TRAIL NAME**                                      **DATE**

**AREA**

**HIKING PARTNER(S)**


**MILEAGE**

**ELEVATION CHANGE**

**HIGH POINT**

**TRAILHEAD GPS COORDINATES**


**TRAIL AND WEATHER CONDITIONS**




**SPOTTED ALONG THE WAY**




**GENERAL NOTES**

TRAIL NAME _____ DATE _____

AREA _____

HIKING PARTNER(S) _____

MILEAGE _____

ELEVATION CHANGE _____

HIGH POINT _____

TRAILHEAD GPS COORDINATES _____

TRAIL AND WEATHER CONDITIONS _____

_____

_____

SPOTTED ALONG THE WAY _____

_____

_____

_____

GENERAL NOTES _____

_____

_____

_____

_____

_____

_____

_____

_____

_____

_____

_____

_____

_____

_____

_____

**TRAIL NAME**                                    DATE

**AREA**

**HIKING PARTNER(S)**


**MILEAGE**

**ELEVATION CHANGE**

**HIGH POINT**

**TRAILHEAD GPS COORDINATES**


**TRAIL AND WEATHER CONDITIONS**


**SPOTTED ALONG THE WAY**


**GENERAL NOTES**

TRAIL NAME

DATE

AREA

HIKING PARTNER(S)

MILEAGE

ELEVATION CHANGE

HIGH POINT

TRAILHEAD GPS COORDINATES

TRAIL AND WEATHER CONDITIONS

SPOTTED ALONG THE WAY

GENERAL NOTES

**TRAIL NAME**                                    DATE

**AREA**

**HIKING PARTNER(S)**


**MILEAGE**

**ELEVATION CHANGE**

**HIGH POINT**

**TRAILHEAD GPS COORDINATES**


**TRAIL AND WEATHER CONDITIONS**



**SPOTTED ALONG THE WAY**




**GENERAL NOTES**

**TRAIL NAME**

**DATE**

**AREA**

**HIKING PARTNER(S)**

**MILEAGE**

**ELEVATION CHANGE**

**HIGH POINT**

**TRAILHEAD GPS COORDINATES**

**TRAIL AND WEATHER CONDITIONS**

**SPOTTED ALONG THE WAY**

**GENERAL NOTES**

**TRAIL NAME**

**DATE**

**AREA**

**HIKING PARTNER(S)**

**MILEAGE**

**ELEVATION CHANGE**

**HIGH POINT**

**TRAILHEAD GPS COORDINATES**

**TRAIL AND WEATHER CONDITIONS**

**SPOTTED ALONG THE WAY**

**GENERAL NOTES**

**TRAIL NAME** _____ **DATE** _____

**AREA** _____

**HIKING PARTNER(S)** _____

**MILEAGE** _____

**ELEVATION CHANGE** _____

**HIGH POINT** _____

**TRAILHEAD GPS COORDINATES** _____

**TRAIL AND WEATHER CONDITIONS** _____
_____

**SPOTTED ALONG THE WAY** _____
_____
_____

**GENERAL NOTES** _____
_____
_____
_____
_____
_____
_____
_____
_____
_____
_____
_____
_____
_____
_____

**TRAIL NAME**

**DATE**

**AREA**

**HIKING PARTNER(S)**

**MILEAGE**

**ELEVATION CHANGE**

**HIGH POINT**

**TRAILHEAD GPS COORDINATES**

**TRAIL AND WEATHER CONDITIONS**

**SPOTTED ALONG THE WAY**

**GENERAL NOTES**

**TRAIL NAME**

**DATE**

**AREA**

**HIKING PARTNER(S)**

**MILEAGE**

**ELEVATION CHANGE**

**HIGH POINT**

**TRAILHEAD GPS COORDINATES**

**TRAIL AND WEATHER CONDITIONS**

**SPOTTED ALONG THE WAY**

**GENERAL NOTES**

**TRAIL NAME**

**DATE**

**AREA**

**HIKING PARTNER(S)**

**MILEAGE**

**ELEVATION CHANGE**

**HIGH POINT**

**TRAILHEAD GPS COORDINATES**

**TRAIL AND WEATHER CONDITIONS**

**SPOTTED ALONG THE WAY**

**GENERAL NOTES**

**TRAIL NAME**                                          **DATE**

**AREA**

**HIKING PARTNER(S)**

**MILEAGE**

**ELEVATION CHANGE**

**HIGH POINT**

**TRAILHEAD GPS COORDINATES**

**TRAIL AND WEATHER CONDITIONS**

**SPOTTED ALONG THE WAY**

**GENERAL NOTES**

TRAIL NAME

DATE

AREA

HIKING PARTNER(S)

MILEAGE

ELEVATION CHANGE

HIGH POINT

TRAILHEAD GPS COORDINATES

TRAIL AND WEATHER CONDITIONS

SPOTTED ALONG THE WAY

GENERAL NOTES

**TRAIL NAME**

**DATE**

**AREA**

**HIKING PARTNER(S)**

**MILEAGE**

**ELEVATION CHANGE**

**HIGH POINT**

**TRAILHEAD GPS COORDINATES**

**TRAIL AND WEATHER CONDITIONS**

**SPOTTED ALONG THE WAY**

**GENERAL NOTES**

**TRAIL NAME**                                          **DATE**

**AREA**

**HIKING PARTNER(S)**

**MILEAGE**

**ELEVATION CHANGE**

**HIGH POINT**

**TRAILHEAD GPS COORDINATES**

**TRAIL AND WEATHER CONDITIONS**

**SPOTTED ALONG THE WAY**

**GENERAL NOTES**

**TRAIL NAME**                                    **DATE**

**AREA**

**HIKING PARTNER(S)**


**MILEAGE**

**ELEVATION CHANGE**

**HIGH POINT**

**TRAILHEAD GPS COORDINATES**


**TRAIL AND WEATHER CONDITIONS**



**SPOTTED ALONG THE WAY**




**GENERAL NOTES**

**TRAIL NAME**                                        **DATE**

**AREA**

**HIKING PARTNER(S)**

**MILEAGE**

**ELEVATION CHANGE**

**HIGH POINT**

**TRAILHEAD GPS COORDINATES**

**TRAIL AND WEATHER CONDITIONS**

**SPOTTED ALONG THE WAY**

**GENERAL NOTES**

**TRAIL NAME**                                    **DATE**

**AREA**

**HIKING PARTNER(S)**


**MILEAGE**

**ELEVATION CHANGE**

**HIGH POINT**

**TRAILHEAD GPS COORDINATES**


**TRAIL AND WEATHER CONDITIONS**


**SPOTTED ALONG THE WAY**


**GENERAL NOTES**

**TRAIL NAME** _____ **DATE** _____

**AREA** _____

**HIKING PARTNER(S)** _____

**MILEAGE** _____

**ELEVATION CHANGE** _____

**HIGH POINT** _____

**TRAILHEAD GPS COORDINATES** _____

**TRAIL AND WEATHER CONDITIONS** _____

_____

**SPOTTED ALONG THE WAY** _____

_____

_____

**GENERAL NOTES** _____

_____

_____

_____

_____

_____

_____

_____

_____

_____

_____

_____

_____

_____

**TRAIL NAME**                                          **DATE**

**AREA**

**HIKING PARTNER(S)**


**MILEAGE**

**ELEVATION CHANGE**

**HIGH POINT**

**TRAILHEAD GPS COORDINATES**


**TRAIL AND WEATHER CONDITIONS**


**SPOTTED ALONG THE WAY**


**GENERAL NOTES**

**TRAIL NAME**                                    **DATE**

**AREA**

**HIKING PARTNER(S)**


**MILEAGE**

**ELEVATION CHANGE**

**HIGH POINT**

**TRAILHEAD GPS COORDINATES**


**TRAIL AND WEATHER CONDITIONS**


**SPOTTED ALONG THE WAY**


**GENERAL NOTES**

**TRAIL NAME**                                        **DATE**

**AREA**

**HIKING PARTNER(S)**


**MILEAGE**

**ELEVATION CHANGE**

**HIGH POINT**

**TRAILHEAD GPS COORDINATES**


**TRAIL AND WEATHER CONDITIONS**


**SPOTTED ALONG THE WAY**


**GENERAL NOTES**

**TRAIL NAME** _____  **DATE** _____

**AREA** _____

**HIKING PARTNER(S)** _____

**MILEAGE** _____

**ELEVATION CHANGE** _____

**HIGH POINT** _____

**TRAILHEAD GPS COORDINATES** _____

**TRAIL AND WEATHER CONDITIONS** _____

_____

_____

**SPOTTED ALONG THE WAY** _____

_____

_____

_____

**GENERAL NOTES** _____

_____

_____

_____

_____

_____

_____

_____

_____

_____

_____

_____

_____

_____

**TRAIL NAME**

**DATE**

**AREA**

**HIKING PARTNER(S)**

**MILEAGE**

**ELEVATION CHANGE**

**HIGH POINT**

**TRAILHEAD GPS COORDINATES**

**TRAIL AND WEATHER CONDITIONS**

**SPOTTED ALONG THE WAY**

**GENERAL NOTES**

**TRAIL NAME**

**DATE**

**AREA**

**HIKING PARTNER(S)**

**MILEAGE**

**ELEVATION CHANGE**

**HIGH POINT**

**TRAILHEAD GPS COORDINATES**

**TRAIL AND WEATHER CONDITIONS**

**SPOTTED ALONG THE WAY**

**GENERAL NOTES**

**TRAIL NAME**

**DATE**

**AREA**

**HIKING PARTNER(S)**

**MILEAGE**

**ELEVATION CHANGE**

**HIGH POINT**

**TRAILHEAD GPS COORDINATES**

**TRAIL AND WEATHER CONDITIONS**

**SPOTTED ALONG THE WAY**

**GENERAL NOTES**

**TRAIL NAME**                                    **DATE**

**AREA**

**HIKING PARTNER(S)**


**MILEAGE**

**ELEVATION CHANGE**

**HIGH POINT**

**TRAILHEAD GPS COORDINATES**


**TRAIL AND WEATHER CONDITIONS**



**SPOTTED ALONG THE WAY**




**GENERAL NOTES**

**TRAIL NAME**

**DATE**

**AREA**

**HIKING PARTNER(S)**

**MILEAGE**

**ELEVATION CHANGE**

**HIGH POINT**

**TRAILHEAD GPS COORDINATES**

**TRAIL AND WEATHER CONDITIONS**

**SPOTTED ALONG THE WAY**

**GENERAL NOTES**

**TRAIL NAME**
_____ **DATE** _____

**AREA**
_____

**HIKING PARTNER(S)**
_____

**MILEAGE**
_____

**ELEVATION CHANGE**
_____

**HIGH POINT**
_____

**TRAILHEAD GPS COORDINATES**
_____

**TRAIL AND WEATHER CONDITIONS**
_____
_____
_____

**SPOTTED ALONG THE WAY**
_____
_____
_____

**GENERAL NOTES**
_____
_____
_____
_____
_____
_____
_____
_____
_____
_____
_____
_____
_____
_____

**TRAIL NAME**

**DATE**

**AREA**

**HIKING PARTNER(S)**

**MILEAGE**

**ELEVATION CHANGE**

**HIGH POINT**

**TRAILHEAD GPS COORDINATES**

**TRAIL AND WEATHER CONDITIONS**

**SPOTTED ALONG THE WAY**

**GENERAL NOTES**

**TRAIL NAME**                                    **DATE**

**AREA**

**HIKING PARTNER(S)**


**MILEAGE**

**ELEVATION CHANGE**

**HIGH POINT**

**TRAILHEAD GPS COORDINATES**


**TRAIL AND WEATHER CONDITIONS**


**SPOTTED ALONG THE WAY**


**GENERAL NOTES**

TRAIL NAME _____ DATE _____

AREA _____

HIKING PARTNER(S) _____

MILEAGE _____

ELEVATION CHANGE _____

HIGH POINT _____

TRAILHEAD GPS COORDINATES _____

TRAIL AND WEATHER CONDITIONS _____

_____

SPOTTED ALONG THE WAY _____

_____

_____

GENERAL NOTES _____

_____

_____

_____

_____

_____

_____

_____

_____

_____

_____

_____

_____

**TRAIL NAME**                                    **DATE**

**AREA**

**HIKING PARTNER(S)**


**MILEAGE**

**ELEVATION CHANGE**

**HIGH POINT**

**TRAILHEAD GPS COORDINATES**


**TRAIL AND WEATHER CONDITIONS**


**SPOTTED ALONG THE WAY**


**GENERAL NOTES**

**TRAIL NAME** _____ **DATE** _____

**AREA** _____

**HIKING PARTNER(S)** _____
_____

**MILEAGE** _____

**ELEVATION CHANGE** _____

**HIGH POINT** _____

**TRAILHEAD GPS COORDINATES** _____
_____

**TRAIL AND WEATHER CONDITIONS** _____
_____
_____

**SPOTTED ALONG THE WAY** _____
_____
_____
_____

**GENERAL NOTES** _____
_____
_____
_____
_____
_____
_____
_____
_____
_____
_____
_____
_____
_____
_____

**TRAIL NAME** _____ **DATE** _____

**AREA** _____

**HIKING PARTNER(S)** _____

_____

**MILEAGE** _____

**ELEVATION CHANGE** _____

**HIGH POINT** _____

**TRAILHEAD GPS COORDINATES** _____

_____

**TRAIL AND WEATHER CONDITIONS** _____

_____

_____

**SPOTTED ALONG THE WAY** _____

_____

_____

_____

**GENERAL NOTES** _____

_____

_____

_____

_____

_____

_____

_____

_____

_____

_____

_____

_____

_____

_____

**TRAIL NAME**                                     **DATE**

**AREA**

**HIKING PARTNER(S)**

**MILEAGE**

**ELEVATION CHANGE**

**HIGH POINT**

**TRAILHEAD GPS COORDINATES**

**TRAIL AND WEATHER CONDITIONS**

**SPOTTED ALONG THE WAY**

**GENERAL NOTES**

**TRAIL NAME**                                              **DATE**

**AREA**

**HIKING PARTNER(S)**


**MILEAGE**

**ELEVATION CHANGE**

**HIGH POINT**

**TRAILHEAD GPS COORDINATES**


**TRAIL AND WEATHER CONDITIONS**


**SPOTTED ALONG THE WAY**


**GENERAL NOTES**

TRAIL NAME _____ DATE _____

AREA _____

HIKING PARTNER(S) _____

_____

MILEAGE _____

ELEVATION CHANGE _____

HIGH POINT _____

TRAILHEAD GPS COORDINATES _____

_____

TRAIL AND WEATHER CONDITIONS _____

_____

_____

SPOTTED ALONG THE WAY _____

_____

_____

_____

GENERAL NOTES _____

_____

_____

_____

_____

_____

_____

_____

_____

_____

_____

_____

_____

TRAIL NAME _____  DATE _____

AREA _____

HIKING PARTNER(S) _____

_____

MILEAGE _____

ELEVATION CHANGE _____

HIGH POINT _____

TRAILHEAD GPS COORDINATES _____

_____

TRAIL AND WEATHER CONDITIONS _____

_____

_____

SPOTTED ALONG THE WAY _____

_____

_____

_____

GENERAL NOTES _____

_____

_____

_____

_____

_____

_____

_____

_____

_____

_____

_____

_____

_____

**TRAIL NAME**                                          **DATE**

**AREA**

**HIKING PARTNER(S)**

**MILEAGE**

**ELEVATION CHANGE**

**HIGH POINT**

**TRAILHEAD GPS COORDINATES**

**TRAIL AND WEATHER CONDITIONS**

**SPOTTED ALONG THE WAY**

**GENERAL NOTES**

**TRAIL NAME** _____  **DATE** _____

**AREA** _____

**HIKING PARTNER(S)** _____

**MILEAGE** _____

**ELEVATION CHANGE** _____

**HIGH POINT** _____

**TRAILHEAD GPS COORDINATES** _____

**TRAIL AND WEATHER CONDITIONS** _____

_____

_____

**SPOTTED ALONG THE WAY** _____

_____

_____

**GENERAL NOTES** _____

_____

_____

_____

_____

_____

_____

_____

_____

_____

_____

_____

_____

_____

_____

**TRAIL NAME**

**DATE**

**AREA**

**HIKING PARTNER(S)**

**MILEAGE**

**ELEVATION CHANGE**

**HIGH POINT**

**TRAILHEAD GPS COORDINATES**

**TRAIL AND WEATHER CONDITIONS**

**SPOTTED ALONG THE WAY**

**GENERAL NOTES**

**TRAIL NAME**

**DATE**

**AREA**

**HIKING PARTNER(S)**

**MILEAGE**

**ELEVATION CHANGE**

**HIGH POINT**

**TRAILHEAD GPS COORDINATES**

**TRAIL AND WEATHER CONDITIONS**

**SPOTTED ALONG THE WAY**

**GENERAL NOTES**

**TRAIL NAME**

**DATE**

**AREA**

**HIKING PARTNER(S)**

**MILEAGE**

**ELEVATION CHANGE**

**HIGH POINT**

**TRAILHEAD GPS COORDINATES**

**TRAIL AND WEATHER CONDITIONS**

**SPOTTED ALONG THE WAY**

**GENERAL NOTES**

**TRAIL NAME**

**DATE**

**AREA**

**HIKING PARTNER(S)**

**MILEAGE**

**ELEVATION CHANGE**

**HIGH POINT**

**TRAILHEAD GPS COORDINATES**

**TRAIL AND WEATHER CONDITIONS**

**SPOTTED ALONG THE WAY**

**GENERAL NOTES**

**TRAIL NAME**                                         **DATE**

**AREA**

**HIKING PARTNER(S)**

**MILEAGE**

**ELEVATION CHANGE**

**HIGH POINT**

**TRAILHEAD GPS COORDINATES**

**TRAIL AND WEATHER CONDITIONS**

**SPOTTED ALONG THE WAY**

**GENERAL NOTES**

**TRAIL NAME**

**DATE**

**AREA**

**HIKING PARTNER(S)**

**MILEAGE**

**ELEVATION CHANGE**

**HIGH POINT**

**TRAILHEAD GPS COORDINATES**

**TRAIL AND WEATHER CONDITIONS**

**SPOTTED ALONG THE WAY**

**GENERAL NOTES**

**TRAIL NAME**                                            **DATE**

**AREA**

**HIKING PARTNER(S)**


**MILEAGE**

**ELEVATION CHANGE**

**HIGH POINT**

**TRAILHEAD GPS COORDINATES**


**TRAIL AND WEATHER CONDITIONS**


**SPOTTED ALONG THE WAY**


**GENERAL NOTES**

**TRAIL NAME** _____  **DATE** _____

**AREA** _____

**HIKING PARTNER(S)** _____

_____

**MILEAGE** _____

**ELEVATION CHANGE** _____

**HIGH POINT** _____

**TRAILHEAD GPS COORDINATES** _____

_____

**TRAIL AND WEATHER CONDITIONS** _____

_____

_____

**SPOTTED ALONG THE WAY** _____

_____

_____

_____

**GENERAL NOTES** _____

_____

_____

_____

_____

_____

_____

_____

_____

_____

_____

_____

_____

_____

**TRAIL NAME** _____     **DATE** _____

**AREA** _____

**HIKING PARTNER(S)** _____

_____

**MILEAGE** _____

**ELEVATION CHANGE** _____

**HIGH POINT** _____

**TRAILHEAD GPS COORDINATES** _____

_____

**TRAIL AND WEATHER CONDITIONS** _____

_____

_____

**SPOTTED ALONG THE WAY** _____

_____

_____

_____

**GENERAL NOTES** _____

_____

_____

_____

_____

_____

_____

_____

_____

_____

_____

_____

_____

_____

**TRAIL NAME** _____ **DATE** _____

**AREA** _____

**HIKING PARTNER(S)** _____

_____

**MILEAGE** _____

**ELEVATION CHANGE** _____

**HIGH POINT** _____

**TRAILHEAD GPS COORDINATES** _____

_____

**TRAIL AND WEATHER CONDITIONS** _____

_____

_____

**SPOTTED ALONG THE WAY** _____

_____

_____

_____

**GENERAL NOTES** _____

_____

_____

_____

_____

_____

_____

_____

_____

_____

_____

_____

_____

_____

TRAIL NAME                                          DATE

AREA

HIKING PARTNER(S)


MILEAGE

ELEVATION CHANGE

HIGH POINT

TRAILHEAD GPS COORDINATES


TRAIL AND WEATHER CONDITIONS



SPOTTED ALONG THE WAY



GENERAL NOTES

TRAIL NAME                                      DATE

AREA

HIKING PARTNER(S)


MILEAGE

ELEVATION CHANGE

HIGH POINT

TRAILHEAD GPS COORDINATES


TRAIL AND WEATHER CONDITIONS


SPOTTED ALONG THE WAY


GENERAL NOTES

TRAIL NAME _____  DATE _____

AREA _____

HIKING PARTNER(S) _____

MILEAGE _____

ELEVATION CHANGE _____

HIGH POINT _____

TRAILHEAD GPS COORDINATES _____

TRAIL AND WEATHER CONDITIONS _____

SPOTTED ALONG THE WAY _____

GENERAL NOTES _____

**TRAIL NAME**

**DATE**

**AREA**

**HIKING PARTNER(S)**

**MILEAGE**

**ELEVATION CHANGE**

**HIGH POINT**

**TRAILHEAD GPS COORDINATES**

**TRAIL AND WEATHER CONDITIONS**

**SPOTTED ALONG THE WAY**

**GENERAL NOTES**

TRAIL NAME _____  DATE _____

AREA _____

HIKING PARTNER(S) _____


MILEAGE _____

ELEVATION CHANGE _____

HIGH POINT _____

TRAILHEAD GPS COORDINATES _____


TRAIL AND WEATHER CONDITIONS _____

_____


SPOTTED ALONG THE WAY _____

_____

_____


GENERAL NOTES _____

_____

_____

_____

_____

_____

_____

_____

_____

_____

_____

_____

_____

TRAIL NAME _____ DATE _____

AREA _____

HIKING PARTNER(S) _____


MILEAGE _____

ELEVATION CHANGE _____

HIGH POINT _____

TRAILHEAD GPS COORDINATES _____


TRAIL AND WEATHER CONDITIONS _____

_____

_____


SPOTTED ALONG THE WAY _____

_____

_____

_____


GENERAL NOTES _____

_____

_____

_____

_____

_____

_____

_____

_____

_____

_____

_____

_____

_____

**TRAIL NAME**

**DATE**

**AREA**

**HIKING PARTNER(S)**

**MILEAGE**

**ELEVATION CHANGE**

**HIGH POINT**

**TRAILHEAD GPS COORDINATES**

**TRAIL AND WEATHER CONDITIONS**

**SPOTTED ALONG THE WAY**

**GENERAL NOTES**

**TRAIL NAME**

**DATE**

**AREA**

**HIKING PARTNER(S)**

**MILEAGE**

**ELEVATION CHANGE**

**HIGH POINT**

**TRAILHEAD GPS COORDINATES**

**TRAIL AND WEATHER CONDITIONS**

**SPOTTED ALONG THE WAY**

**GENERAL NOTES**

**TRAIL NAME** _____ **DATE** _____

**AREA** _____

**HIKING PARTNER(S)** _____

**MILEAGE** _____

**ELEVATION CHANGE** _____

**HIGH POINT** _____

**TRAILHEAD GPS COORDINATES** _____

**TRAIL AND WEATHER CONDITIONS** _____

_____

**SPOTTED ALONG THE WAY** _____

_____

_____

**GENERAL NOTES** _____

_____

_____

_____

_____

_____

_____

_____

_____

_____

_____

_____

_____

_____

**TRAIL NAME**                                              **DATE**

**AREA**

**HIKING PARTNER(S)**

**MILEAGE**

**ELEVATION CHANGE**

**HIGH POINT**

**TRAILHEAD GPS COORDINATES**

**TRAIL AND WEATHER CONDITIONS**

**SPOTTED ALONG THE WAY**

**GENERAL NOTES**

**TRAIL NAME**                                  **DATE**

**AREA**

**HIKING PARTNER(S)**


**MILEAGE**

**ELEVATION CHANGE**

**HIGH POINT**

**TRAILHEAD GPS COORDINATES**


**TRAIL AND WEATHER CONDITIONS**


**SPOTTED ALONG THE WAY**


**GENERAL NOTES**

**MOUNTAINEERS BOOKS**
Enjoy your hiking adventures. And remember to Leave No Trace, www.lnt.org

ISBN 978-1-68051-324-0

*An independent nonprofit publisher since 1960*